MOSQUITOES

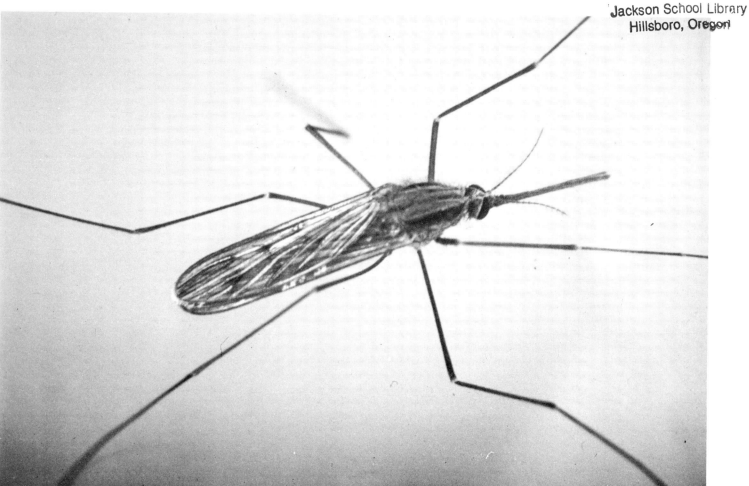

Dorothy Hinshaw Patent

HOLIDAY HOUSE / NEW YORK

Library of Congress Cataloging-in-Publication Data

Patent, Dorothy Hinshaw.
    Mosquitoes.

Includes index.
SUMMARY: discusses the mosquito's habits,
development, and diseases it carries, as well as ways
to control these creatures.
    1. Mosquitoes—Juvenile literature.   [1. Mosquitoes]
I. Title.
QL536.P38   1986   595.77′1   86-45387
ISBN 0-8234-0627-X

FRONTISPIECE ILLUSTRATION COURTESY
DEPARTMENT OF ENTOMOLOGY,
UNIVERSITY OF MARYLAND

Contents

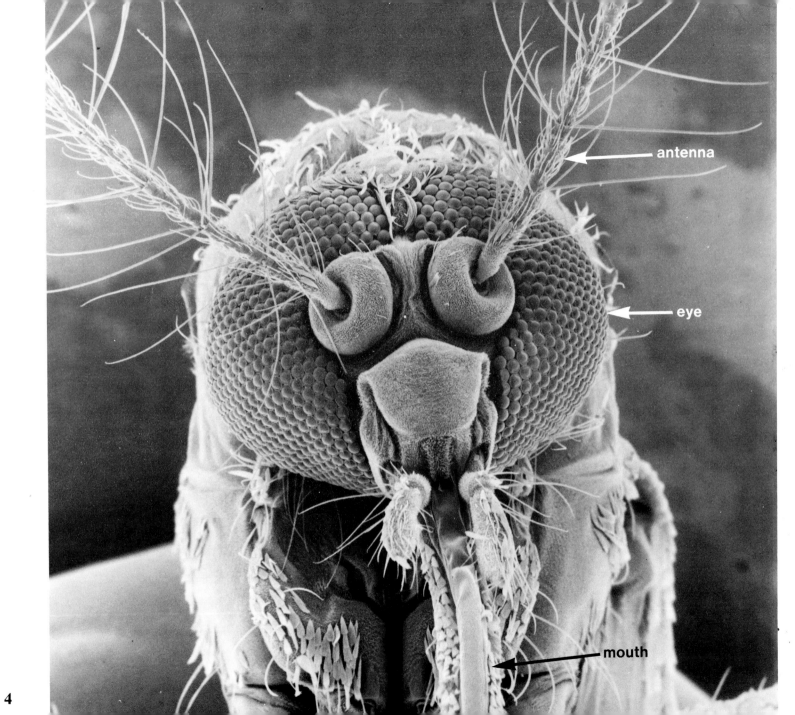

antenna

eye

mouth

4

Mosquitoes

Itch, itch, scratch. It's summertime, and the mosquitoes are at it again. They bite us and feed on our blood. We may not like these tiny insects, but we should respect them. They are small and delicate looking, but mosquitoes are very hard to get rid of. They live just about everywhere people do, so almost no one is free of them. They attack other living things, too, including birds, frogs, and dogs. Some mosquitoes even get their food by stealing it from ants. Altogether, there are more than 2,500 sorts of mosquitoes. About 130 kinds live in North America. Most of them never bite people, and some just feed on fruit and flowers, never blood.

Mosquitoes not only bite and make us itch, they can also make people very sick. In many parts of the world, millions of dollars are spent each year trying to stop the diseases mosquitoes carry.

This magnified photograph shows the face of a female mosquito. The sucking mouth sticks out in front. The two bristly antennae point out toward the sides. The big eyes behind the antennae look like bunches of small bumps.

RALPH E. HARBACH. PHOTO COURTESY
NATIONAL MUSEUM OF NATURAL HISTORY

The Larva

While adult mosquitoes fly through the air, young mosquitoes live in the water. The female mosquito lays her eggs on the water's surface. Some have eggs that float separately. Others make tiny rafts of eggs that stay together until they hatch. The little animal that comes out of the egg looks nothing like a grown-up mosquito. It is called a larva.

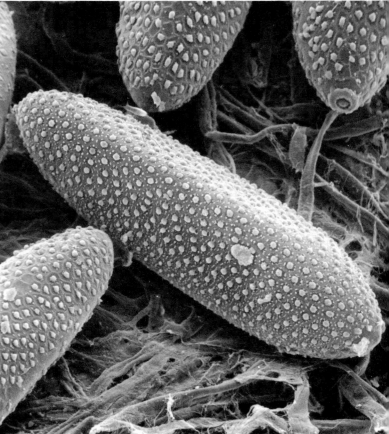

These mosquito eggs are magnified many times their real size.
RALPH E. HARBACH

A raft of mosquito eggs. EUGENE J. GERBERG

air tube

Two mosquito larvae in the water, hanging with their heads down. You can see the tubes that take in air.
EUGENE J. GERBERG

The larva has no legs or wings, but it does have a pair of eyes on its head. Even though the larva lives in the water, it breathes air. Near the tail end of its body is an opening that takes in air from above the surface. The larvae of many common mosquitoes have an air tube extending to the surface. These larvae hang head downward in the water. Other larvae do not have a tube. They lie just below the surface, where they feed on small particles of food.

When the larva feeds, it uses about a thousand tiny bristles alongside its mouth to sweep in small bits of food. The bristles move fast, raking the water several times each second. The body of the larva has longer bristles that help sense touch and movement in the water.

The magnified face of a mosquito larva. The many fine bristles are used to sweep food into the mouth. RALPH E. HARBACH

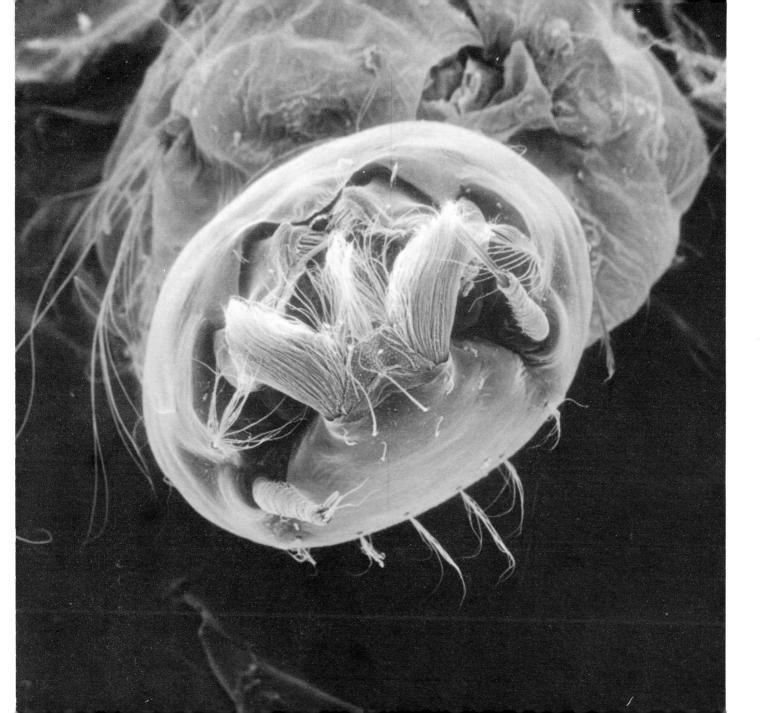

9

When the larva feeds or rests, it keeps the air opening in touch with the water's surface. But if a shadow passes across the water or if the larva is disturbed, it lives up to its common name, wiggler. It wiggles its way quickly to the bottom. There it rests until things quiet down. The air opening closes automatically when the larva goes under water.

Mosquitoes do not spend much time as wigglers. They grow fast and shed their tough outer covering, called the cuticle (CUTE-i-cul) three times in a few days. During the last larval stage, the wiggler changes. New body parts develop under the cuticle, and the larva grows fast. It is getting ready for the next stage in its life.

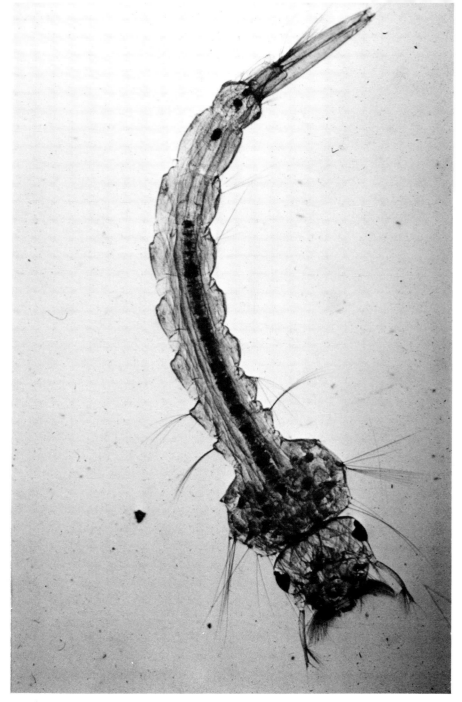

When a mosquito larva senses danger, it leaves the water's surface. Here you can see the feeding bristles, antennae, and eyes on the head. The larva is so transparent that you can see food inside its intestine, too.

DEPARTMENT OF ENTOMOLOGY,
UNIVERSITY OF MARYLAND

The Pupa

When the larva sheds its cuticle for the last time, a very different creature comes out. It is called the pupa (PEW-pah). The pupa looks like a fat comma with ears. The "ears" are a pair of breathing tubes near the head end. The pupa floats at the surface, held there by an air bubble in its body. It has no mouth and does not eat. At the tail end, the pupa has a pair of paddles used to wiggle to the bottom when danger threatens.

The mosquito lives as a pupa for several days. If the water dries out, it can still survive in moist air. Within the pupa, big changes are taking place. The old muscles of the larva are broken down, and adult muscles are built up. The digestive system is changed from one that handles small food particles to one that relies on a liquid diet. The wings and the long, sucking mouth develop. The eyes become much bigger and better able to see.

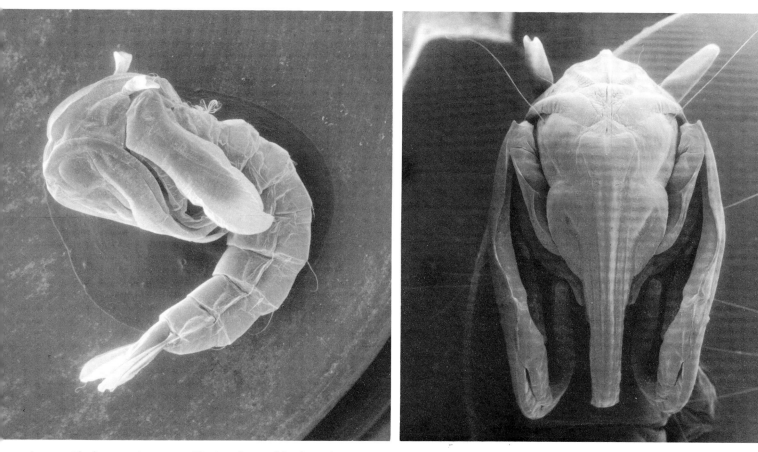

A magnified mosquito pupa. Notice the earlike breathing tubes at the top. These open to the water's surface. If you look closely, you can see the outline of the adult's body. The flap on the side covers a developing wing.
RALPH E. HARBACH

The magnified face of the mosquito pupa. The pupa itself has no eyes. RALPH E. HARBACH

By the time the pupa stage is over, a completely different insect lives inside. Shortly before the pupa breaks open, it darkens in color. It lies straightened out at the water's surface. The back of the cuticle splits open, and the new adult mosquito steadily pulls itself out. At first it looks soft and rather shapeless. But then the cuticle hardens and the wings spread out. After only ten minutes, the young adult mosquito is ready to take a short flight to the shelter of nearby plants to rest.

An adult mosquito pulls herself out of the pupa. Soon the legs will step out and the wings will spread and harden. EDWARD S. ROSS

15

The Adult Mosquito

Like other insects, a mosquito has a body with three parts—a head, a thorax, and an abdomen. The head has a large pair of eyes and a pair of antennae that reach forward and help the mosquito sense its world. The mosquito's mouth is long and thin, for sucking up nectar and blood. On the thorax is a pair of thin, delicate-looking wings and six long, slender legs. Most of the body organs are inside the long abdomen.

After resting for a day or two, the young mosquito ventures out for its first meal. It does not look for blood. Instead it feeds on the sweet liquid in flowers, called nectar. Mosquitoes feed mainly at dusk or during the night.

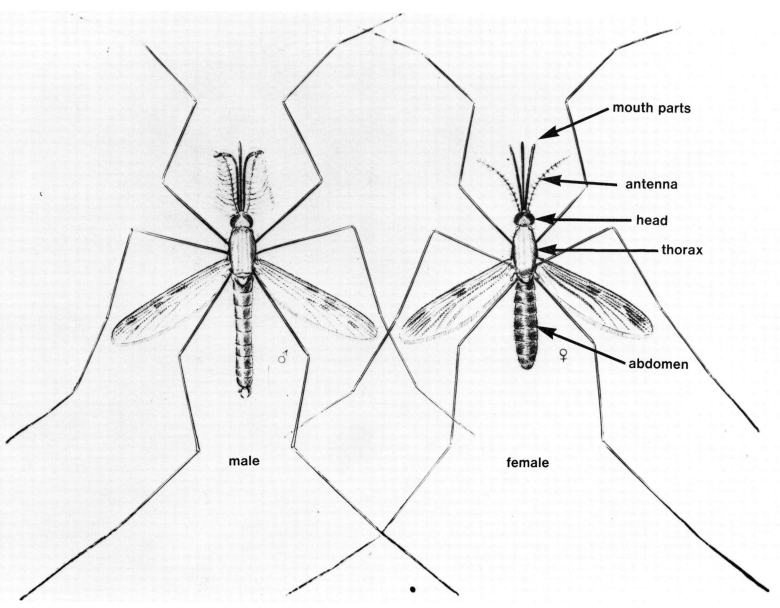

mouth parts

antenna

head

thorax

abdomen

male

female

Male and female mosquitoes. The separate parts of the mouth are spread out in these drawings. USDA PHOTO

17

Soon the young mosquitoes are ready to mate. The male's antennae are thick with long hairs. These hairs are sensitive to the whining sound made by the female's wings when she flies. The male is attracted by the sound. When a male finds a female, they mate. The female stores the male's sperm in her body.

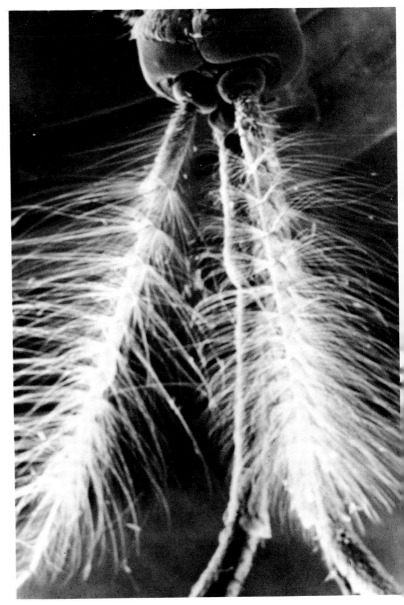

This magnified photo shows the many hairs on the antenna of a male mosquito.
NEW ORLEANS MOSQUITO CONTROL

*Mosquitoes have plenty of enemies. Here a mosquito
larva is attacked by two fly larvae.* EDWARD S. ROSS

Life for a mosquito is full of danger. Many water insects eat
mosquito larvae, and fungi and viruses can also kill them. Once
the mosquito emerges into the air, birds, bats, spiders, lizards, and
other creatures may make a meal of it. Each day, almost a third of
the mosquitoes in the world might die. Only about one in every
two hundred survives to reproduce. A mosquito lucky enough to
escape enemies can live as long as five months.

Feeding on Blood

Both the male and the female mosquito feed on nectar. The females of most kinds also bite animals and suck their blood. They need the protein in the blood so that their bodies can manufacture eggs.

The mosquito finds its victim, or host, by sensing the warm, moist air around the body. It is also sensitive to carbon dioxide, a gas that is released when animals breathe. After it finds a host to bite, the mosquito lands gently. Since it only weighs 1/25,000 ounce, it is usually impossible to feel the mosquito as it touches down.

This magnified picture shows the delicate foot of a mosquito.
RALPH E. HARBACH

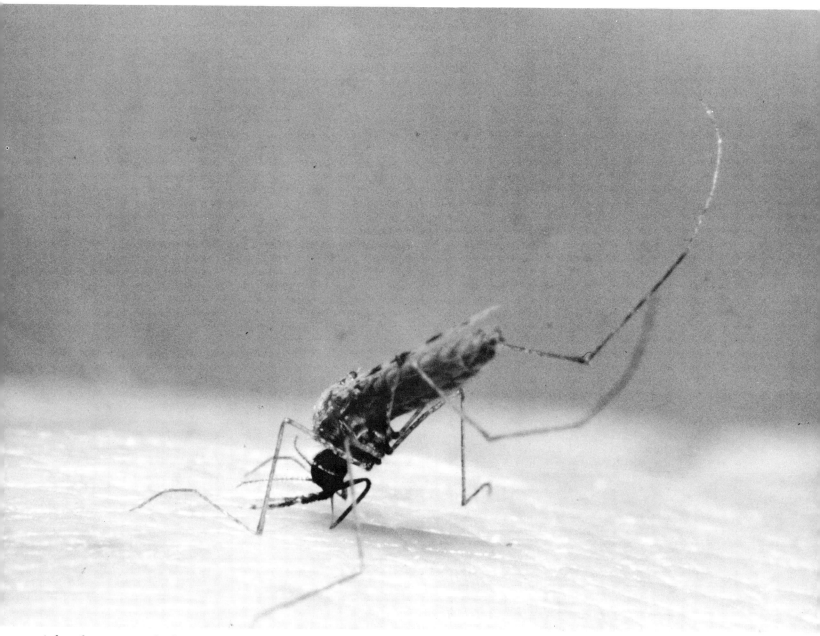

A female mosquito feeding. EUGENE J. GERBERG

The biting mouth, called the proboscis (pro-BAH-sis), of the female mosquito has several parts. In the center are two very slender tubes. Saliva flows through one tube into the bite. Blood is sucked into the mouth through the other. Around the tubes are two pairs of cutting tools that pierce the skin during the bite. All these parts, called stylets, rest in the groove of a protective sheath, named the labium (LAY-bee-um).

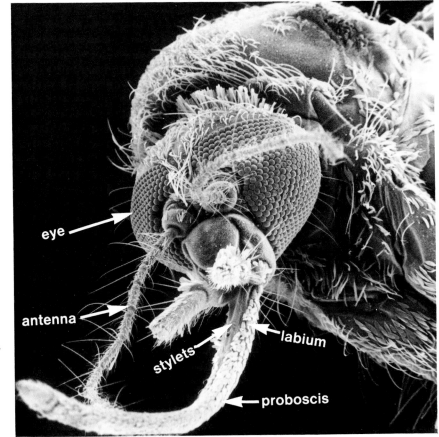

The proboscis of this magnified female mosquito is bent. If you look closely at the base of the proboscis, you can see the stylets in the groove of the labium.
RALPH E. HARBACH

When the mosquito bites, the tip of the proboscis is pushed against the skin. Then, the cutting tools move up and down, driving the stylets deeper through the skin. The labium stays outside and bends as the stylets penetrate deeper.

The tip is moved this way and that, probing for a tiny blood vessel. When one is reached, the tip slides in. Saliva is pumped into the vessel. It helps increase the blood flow so the mosquito can get its fill quickly. The saliva of some mosquitoes also keeps the blood from clotting.

Within 90 seconds, the mosquito has taken in several times her weight in blood. Her abdomen is stretched and swollen. Usually before the victim can feel the bite, the insect takes off. She now has enough food to help from seventy-five to five hundred eggs develop.

The Telltale Itch

If the mosquito has not finished her meal in two minutes, she is in trouble. By then, her victim is likely to feel an itch, which may mean death to the mosquito. The itch is caused by an allergic reaction to the saliva that was injected. As the host's body reacts to the saliva, it sends extra blood to the site of the bite. Changes in the body cells affected by the bite cause fluid to build up. This results in the swollen, itching bump around the bite.

Some people believe that the itching will be less if the mosquito is left to finish her meal once she is discovered. Supposedly, she sucks back most of the saliva so that the allergic reaction is less. But scientists say this isn't so.

A mosquito finishes off her meal. Her abdomen is swollen with blood. Notice the thick, bent labium and the thinner set of stylets that penetrate the skin. The mosquito is releasing a droplet of liquid from her intestine. By letting out some of the fluid from her blood meal, the mosquito reduces her weight so that it is easier to fly away.
EUGENE J. GERBERG

Eggs of the yellow fever mosquito. The female lays about 100 eggs at one time. EUGENE J. GERBERG

Laying the Eggs

After filling up on blood, the female mosquito flies off to a sheltered place where she rests. The blood is digested and the eggs grow. After a few days, the mosquito takes off in search of a place to lay her eggs. She finds water by looking for spots that appear darker than the area around them.

When she finds a good egg-laying location, the female lands gently on the water. She is so light that she can stand on the surface without getting wet. As the eggs are laid they are fertilized by the stored sperm. When the female is finished, she flies away to begin the cycle of blood feeding and egg laying all over again. If a mosquito avoids being eaten by enemies, she may take in as many as twenty blood meals and lay eggs twenty times. Thus it is possible for one mosquito to lay thousands of eggs before she dies.

Different kinds of mosquitoes lay eggs in different types of places. Some use small, quiet ponds, while others use slowly flowing streams. Very small, still bodies of water are favorites with many mosquitoes. Some even put them in the tiny cavities between the leaves and stems of tropical plants.

Mosquitoes and Disease

Mosquitoes carry many diseases that can make people sick. Most of these diseases only occur in warm, tropical places. Mosquitoes can pick up tiny worms that live in the blood of one person and pass them on to another. Several diseases are spread by mosquitoes, but the two most important are yellow fever and malaria.

Yellow fever is caused by a virus. It is passed from person to person by the yellow fever mosquito, whose scientific name is *Aedes aegypti*. The yellow fever mosquito lives in the warmer parts of the world. It lays its eggs in very small, stagnant puddles of water. Old tires, birdbaths, buckets, roof gutters, empty cans, and so on are favorite sites. It will even leave its eggs in flower vases inside of houses.

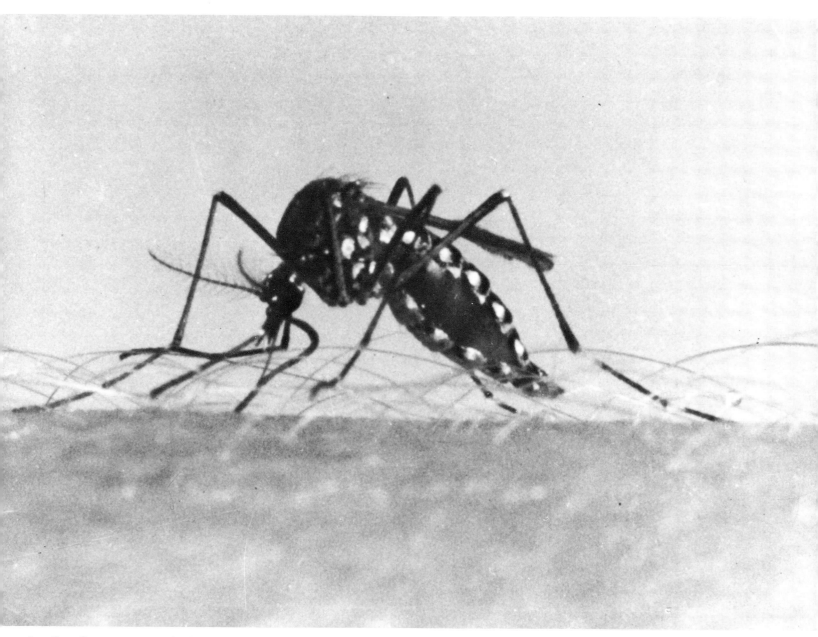

A yellow fever mosquito feeding. USDA PHOTO

William Gorgas, on the left, travels by ship to Havana in 1904 with Ronald Ross. Ross did important research on the life cycle of malaria.

The Panama Canal was almost not built because of the mosquito. Every time work began on the canal, yellow fever killed many of the workers. Then, in 1905, an American army doctor named William Gorgas took over efforts to stop the disease. He had houses sprayed with insecticides and water-filled containers removed. He taught people how to use window screens and mosquito netting to protect themselves. After a few months, yellow fever was almost completely gone from Panama, and the canal could be finished.

An Anopheles *mosquito finishing her meal.* EUGENE J. GERBERG

Malaria

Malaria still endangers the lives of millions of people. It is carried by several kinds of mosquitoes called *Anopheles.* The word "malaria" means "bad air." People once thought it was caused by the air rising from swamps. They thought it could be prevented by sleeping with the windows closed. Sleeping with closed windows can help, of course, because that helps keep mosquitoes out of the house. But it doesn't stop the disease completely.

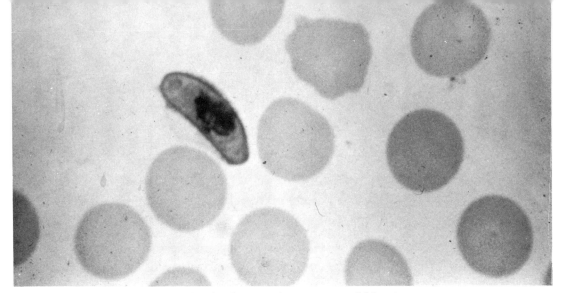

A malaria parasite in the blood. The round spots are red blood cells. The darker, elongated object is the parasite. EUGENE J. GERBERG

Malaria is caused by a single-celled parasite. When an infected mosquito bites a person, the parasites go to the liver and reproduce several times, making many more of them. Next the parasites leave the liver.

Each parasite then enters a red blood cell. Inside the cell, the parasite multiplies again to make sixteen more. The cell breaks open, and the new parasites each enter a different cell. This happens over and over again. The parasites multiply at the same rate so that the cells burst at the same time. When this happens, the sick person gets chills and a high fever.

After several cycles, some of the parasites change. They enter red blood cells just like the others. But instead of dividing there, they become male and female cells. Then if a mosquito bites the sick person, it sucks in some of these cells. Once they enter the mosquito's stomach, the male cells split up into many smaller cells. Each of these can combine with a female cell, fertilizing it to form a zygote (ZI-goat). The zygote buries itself in the wall of the mosquito's stomach. There it divides over and over again, making as many as ten thousand new parasites. After about ten days, the parasites travel to the salivary gland of the mosquito. Now they are ready to infect any people the mosquito bites.

Flowers and leaves of the cinchona tree. EUGENE J. GERBERG

Malaria does not usually kill adults, but it takes away their energy and makes them feel very sick. Children often die from the disease. Malaria is still common in parts of India and Africa. About half the public health budget of India goes to the fight against malaria.

Treating malaria is sometimes difficult. Quinine, which comes from the bark of the cinchona tree, is used against the disease. Similar chemicals made in the laboratory are used, too. But some strains of the malaria parasite are now resistant to these drugs.

Other Diseases Mosquitoes Carry

Of the many illnesses carried by mosquitoes, scientists are worried about two others. One is encephalitis (en-sef-a-LIGHT-us). This disease can cause a high fever and sometimes brain damage or even death. One variety that exists in the United States infects horses. Humans can get a different kind of encephalitis from mosquitos, but that one hasn't become a problem here yet.

The other disease that worries scientists is dengue fever. Dengue makes people very sick for about six weeks. Their joints and back hurt very badly, and they have a fever and a rash. Dengue rarely kills people, but it makes them miserable. It is a big problem in the Caribbean islands now. Doctors are worried that dengue may move into the southeastern United States from the Caribbean.

Scientists keep trying to find new repellents to keep mosquitoes away. But so far, just one chemical, called Deet, really works well. Repellents work by confusing the mosquito. They block the microscopic pores that allow the mosquito to sense the warmth and moisture of the person's body. Repellents only work in an enclosed area or when sprayed or rubbed right on the skin. If you are wearing repellent, mosquitoes may fly close to you, but they won't land and bite.

Mosquito repellent makes it easier
to enjoy summer out-of-doors.
S. C. JOHNSON & SON, INC.

A plane sprays insecticide to control mosquitoes.
CENTERS FOR DISEASE CONTROL

Getting Rid of Mosquitoes

One way to stop malaria and other diseases carried by mosquitoes is to eliminate the mosquitoes themselves. For many years, insecticides such as DDT were sprayed to kill mosquitoes. Now, however, many kinds of mosquitoes are resistant to DDT and other insecticides. New ways must be found to get rid of them.

Fortunately, there are other methods. Eliminating the places where mosquitoes breed works well, when it is possible. Another way is to use natural enemies of disease-carrying mosquitoes to kill them off. One such enemy is a giant mosquito (*Toxorhynchites rutilus rutilus*) whose larvae are almost three times as long as yellow fever mosquito larvae. These larvae eat the smaller larvae, and the females lay their eggs in the same kinds of locations as do yellow fever mosquitoes. Since the adults of the giant mosquito do not bite, they are not a problem for people.

Biting mosquitoes will probably always be with us. But we can hope that those carrying diseases can be eliminated. Then all that people will need to be concerned about is itchy bites, not deadly sickness.

A marsh being sprayed for mosquitoes.
ORANGE COUNTY VECTOR CONTROL DISTRICT,
ORANGE COUNTY, CALIFORNIA

Index